HS A
HOMELAND SEC
OPERATIONAL ANALYSIS

Determining Staffing Needs for Administrative, Professional, and Technical Workers in the U.S. Secret Service

Methods and Lessons Learned

DAVID SCHULKER, NELSON LIM, ALBERT A. ROBBERT

Published in 2020

Preface

This report outlines methodological considerations for a study designed to help the U.S. Secret Service determine staffing needs in a subset of administrative, professional, and technical work functions. The authors analyzed organizational structures, workflows, available data, and operational needs to consider possible approaches to build tools for Secret Service workforce planners to use in making staffing determinations. The report discusses the organizational context of the service, summarizes possible approaches with a rationale for the primary and secondary approaches that the researchers adopted, and discusses implementation considerations and lessons learned for future work. The findings in this report should be of interest to decisionmakers and workforce planners in federal agencies seeking to develop and implement staffing models for their professional workforces.

This research was sponsored by the U.S. Secret Service Workforce Planning Division and conducted within the Personnel and Resources Program of the Homeland Security Operational Analysis Center federally funded research and development center (FFRDC).

About the Homeland Security Operational Analysis Center

The Homeland Security Act of 2002 (Section 305 of Public Law 107-296, as codified at 6 U.S.C. § 185) authorizes the Secretary of Homeland Security, acting through the Under Secretary for Science and Technology, to establish one or more FFRDCs to provide independent analysis of homeland security issues. The RAND Corporation operates HSOAC as an FFRDC for the U.S. Department of Homeland Security (DHS) under contract HSHQDC-16-D-00007.

The HSOAC FFRDC provides the government with independent and objective analyses and advice in core areas important to the department in support of policy development, decisionmaking, alternative approaches, and new ideas on issues of significance. The HSOAC FFRDC also works with and supports other federal, state, local, tribal, and public- and private-sector organizations that make up the homeland security enterprise. The HSOAC FFRDC's research is undertaken by mutual consent with DHS and is organized as a set of discrete tasks. This report presents the results of research and analysis conducted under task 70US0918F1DHS0071, Models for APT Workforce.

The results presented in this report do not necessarily reflect official DHS opinion or policy.

For more information on HSOAC, see www.rand.org/hsoac. For more information on this publication, see www.rand.org/t/RR3206.

Contents

Preface iii
Figures and Tables vii
Summary ix
Acknowledgments xiii
Abbreviations xv

CHAPTER ONE
Introduction 1
The Focus of This Report 3
An Outline of This Report 4

CHAPTER TWO
Selecting the Right Staffing Model 5
Planners Can Use Any of a Variety of Methods for Determining
    Staffing Needs 5
The Bottom-Up Workload Estimator Approach Is the Most Suitable
    Basis for the Staffing Models in the Functions Under Study 10

CHAPTER THREE
Considerations for Implementing Our Primary and Secondary
    Approaches 15
Our Primary Approach: Executing a Bottom-Up Workload Estimator
    Model 15
Our Secondary Approach: Business-Case Analysis 26
Calibrating All Available Information to Arrive at a Staffing Estimate . . . 28

CHAPTER FOUR
Alternative Approaches for Information Technology Functions 31
Software Operations and Maintenance Activities............................32
Software Development Activities.. 34
Applying These Methods to the Applications Development Branch 37
Improving Staffing Approaches for Information Technology
    Functions... 38

CHAPTER FIVE
Lessons Learned for Future Analyses of Staffing Needs 39
Certain Conditions Must Exist to Maximize the Benefit of a Staffing
    Study..39
Even Models with Limited Quantitative Precision Help Make
    Planning More Transparent..41
There Is Benefit to Focused Periods of Model Development...............43
Conclusion 43

References 45

Figures and Tables

Figures

2.1. Diagram of a Generic Staffing Model........................... 6
2.2. An Illustration of an Example Performance Estimator
      Staffing Model 8
3.1. A Conceptual Diagram of Our Bottom-Up Workload
      Approach... 16
3.2. A Process Map of Payroll Military Buyback Activities.......... 18
3.3. A Process Map of Payroll Military Buyback Activities
      with Frequency and Time Estimates 20
3.4. An Example of Incorporating Work Features into a
      Process Map 22
3.5. An Example of the Comparison Between the Number of
      Hours of Overtime Charged and the Number of Hours of
      National Special Security Event–Related Work Required...... 25
5.1. Bottom-Up Models Serve Multiple Workforce Planning
      Functions 42

Tables

2.1. An Overview of the Studied Functions 11
3.1. Potential Approaches for Resourcing National Special
      Security Events... 24
4.1. Sample Performance Statistics for Staffing a Request-
      Driven Workload of 1.8 Full-Time Equivalents.................. 33

Summary

The U.S. Secret Service has historically sized its administrative, professional, and technical (APT) workforce using a ratio that pegs the number of APT employees to the size of the law enforcement population in the organization. Dramatic organizational changes and feedback from managers jointly suggest that these ratios no longer provide a good approximation of APT requirements. In response, the Secret Service Workforce Planning Division requested that the Homeland Security Operational Analysis Center conduct a study to propose new approaches for determining staffing needs in the service's highest-priority APT functions. The study functions included two financial administration functions (the Administrative Operations Division and the Budget Division), one human resource function (the Benefits and Payroll Division), and two information technology functions (the Applications Development Branch and the Communications Branch). To select a suitable staffing approach for each area, the study team conducted discussions with managers and employees to assess patterns of work and available data.

A staffing model is a simplified representation of the process by which inputs, such as workers and technology, produce outputs that are important to an organization's mission. A model that includes a faithful rendering of the output-generating process can also calculate the number of inputs that produce a desired level of output. Potential approaches for modeling staffing requirements are not necessarily quantitative, and they can incorporate subjective assessments based on the strategic perspectives of managers or subject-matter experts. Which modeling approach is the most suitable for a function depends on the organizational structure, workflow, available data sources, and operational needs, such as ease of implementation and adaptability.

In the case of the specific functions included in this study, purely quantitative approaches were not feasible, sometimes because of the workflow structure and sometimes because available data were insufficient. Instead, we applied a bottom-up approach commonly used for staffing models of administrative work that involved constructing process maps for the major work processes that produce each function's outputs and pairing those maps with estimates of the frequency and duration of each process. These bottom-up inputs let us estimate the total workload, which, when combined with other parameters, provides an actionable number of full-time–equivalent employees that will be sufficient to accomplish the function's workload. We also discuss a more subjective approach, known as a business-case analysis, that was occasionally helpful to generate supplemental information or that we used for areas in which the work was too unstructured for the bottom-up approach to yield reliable estimates.

Workflows in the Applications Development Branch were distinctive because of the influence of agile methodologies for project management. Software development activities have moved away from linear, sequential processes and instead rely on iterative workflows (such as scrum methods) that incrementally build products in collaboration with stakeholders. For these areas, we propose some simple, easy-to-implement calculations based on the constructs that the Secret Service uses, as well as more-complex approaches that involve computer simulation and optimization techniques. The more-complex approaches would produce estimates with higher fidelity, but we could not implement them because of data limitations. These techniques are readily available if the service desires refined estimates for software development activities, provided that the organization invests in improvements to data collection procedures.

Finally, our experience with the Secret Service yielded three main lessons learned for future research and other organizations seeking to develop staffing models for APT functions. First, it would have been beneficial to conduct a preliminary assessment of candidate functions to determine whether the functions are ripe for a staffing study. This preliminary assessment would examine whether (1) subject-matter experts have sufficient time to participate in the study, (2) the organizational structure and mission are clearly defined and stable, (3) the work processes in the function are stable and efficient, (4) workflow data on key processes are captured, and (5) performance dimensions are defined and captured in data if possible. In cases in which these criteria are not met, functions could have the opportunity to implement changes before proceeding with developing a model. Second, although the bottom-up models rely on subjective inputs that are difficult to validate, the process of developing them produced additional benefits to workforce planners. Even a potentially noisy bottom-up model yields great increases in transparency in the work activities that decisionmakers are resourcing, for instance. Third, some of our difficulties in implementing the bottom-up approach might be alleviated in future work by earmarking focused study periods instead of attempting to do the study on top of normal work schedules.

There is a sense in which each staffing problem is unique, so any staffing model must be customized to the work context at hand. Federal organizations should continue to capitalize on the increasingly low cost of data collection to provide indicators of staffing sufficiency and inform model development. In the meantime, the methods outlined in this report provide an option to workforce planners for producing decision-quality information on staffing levels in APT work.

Acknowledgments

We are extremely grateful for all of the assistance we received throughout this project. We thank the U.S. Secret Service's chief human capital officer, Susan Yarwood, who sponsored this project. We are also grateful to Thomas Hamann, chief of the Workforce Planning Division (WPL), and Gregory Mills, social research analyst in WPL, for their consistent engagement and assistance in executing the study. We thank Mark Zolecki in WPL for assisting with the various sources of workforce data. Each of the staffing models we developed required significant time commitments from the managers and subject-matter experts in the study functions, and we thank them for their patience and willing participation in the study. We appreciate the efforts of the following managers of the study functions for their collaboration and for enabling these time commitments from their personnel: Nancy Riggins, Wanda Washington, Miki Morrison, David Toth, Corey Beckett, Catrina White-Wilson, Richard Sabo, and Emanuel Cohan, as well as their many section chiefs who collaborated with us extensively in the model development process.

We would also like to thank several people at RAND who were helpful throughout. We thank Jeremy M. Eckhause for his help developing the technical execution plan for this study and Phillip Carter for his consistent help throughout the study. We appreciate the high-quality feedback we received from our reviewers, James R. Broyles, Lisa M. Harrington, and Paul Dreyer. Finally, we appreciate the work of several team members who contributed to efforts to refine and apply our methods: Brandon Crosby, Clara Aranibar, Maria C. Lytell, Susan A. Resetar, Hilary Reininger, Julia Brackup, and Thomas Edward Goode.

Abbreviations

APT   administrative, professional, and technical

BCA   business-case analysis

FTE   full-time equivalent

GAO   U.S. Government Accountability Office

HR   human resource

IT   information technology

NFC   National Finance Center

NSSE   National Special Security Event

O&M   operations and maintenance

SA   special agent

SME   subject-matter expert

UD   Uniformed Division

CHAPTER ONE

Introduction

According to the U.S. Government Accountability Office (GAO), strategic human capital management has been one of the high-risk challenges faced by federal agencies since 2001 (GAO, 2019).[1] GAO contended that the failures of the U.S. Office of Personnel Management and federal agencies to strategically manage the federal workforce could "pose a high risk to the nation because they impede the government from cost-effectively serving the public and achieving results" (GAO, 2019, p. 75). Therefore, GAO recommended that the Office of Personnel Management and federal agencies "continue developing the capacity to measure and address existing mission-critical skills gaps, and use workforce analytics to predict and mitigate future gaps so agencies can effectively carry out their missions" (GAO, 2019, p. 75). Workforce analytics, which include reliable staffing models and tools, are essential elements of effective strategic human capital management (Emmerichs, Marcum, and Robbert, 2004b).

As a federal agency, the U.S. Secret Service also needs to strategically manage its human capital because its workforce management practices have been the subject of considerable scrutiny in recent years, after inquiries in response to several high-profile incidents pointed to workforce challenges as a key contributing factor (National Academy of Public Administration, 2016). For instance, the Secret Service Protective Mission Panel, established in response to a fence-line incursion at

---

[1] GAO's high-risk program is designed to identify "government operations with vulnerabilities to fraud, waste, abuse, and mismanagement, or in need of transformation to address economy, efficiency, or effectiveness challenges" (GAO, 2019, p. 1).

the White House in 2014, reported that more special agents (SAs) and Uniformed Division (UD) officers were needed at the White House complex and that the service needed more "specialized expertise in its budget, workforce, and technology functions" (Hagin et al., 2014, p. 7). This finding, along with those from other reports, prompted a significant reorganization of the administrative, professional, and technical (APT) workforce structure. Furthermore, in response to reports that the existing workforce was undersized, as well as anticipated mission growth, the Secret Service human capital strategic plan aims to grow the total workforce by 2,795 employees (41 percent) from fiscal years 2018 through 2025 by utilizing the full spectrum of hiring, development, and retention activities available to it (U.S. Secret Service, 2017).

The Secret Service fulfills its charge of protecting national leaders and visiting heads of state, as well as securing the U.S. financial system, through criminal investigations utilizing three primary categories of workers: SAs, UD officers, and APT employees. The service determines staffing levels for SAs and UD officers using standardized calculations based on mission requirements. For instance, work requirements in the protection mission area are often based on the number of posts and shifts that agents or officers must fill, plus allowances for normal absences and training. For APT staffing, the service begins with a ratio of one APT employee per 2.5 law enforcement employees, supplemented by incremental increases or decreases using feedback from subject-matter experts (SMEs). Although these simple ratios represent an intuitive and accessible starting point, changes in workforce composition or organization (both of which occurred in the Secret Service in recent years) could cause ratio estimates that have worked well in the past to become inaccurate (Nataraj et al., 2014). Thus, Secret Service workforce managers sought the RAND Corporation's assistance to develop more-reliable staffing models for their highest-priority APT functions, which included two financial administration functions, one human resources (HR) function, and two information technology (IT) functions.

The Focus of This Report

The primary objective of this report is to provide internal, as well as external, Secret Service stakeholders with a strategic overview of the methodological considerations and decisions we made in our effort to develop reliable staffing models for five Secret Service APT functions:

- Administrative Operations Division
- Budget Division
- Benefits and Payroll Division
- Applications Development Branch
- Communications Branch.

This report describes the available methodological options and key considerations for the process of determining staffing levels for these functions. Even though the primary focus of the report is to inform Secret Service stakeholders, other federal agencies who are grappling with the same issues that GAO raised could also benefit from this description of the methods that we chose and the key considerations for implementing them.

This report's scope is intentionally limited to methodological considerations and does not discuss certain aspects of designing and implementing staffing models. For example, we implemented the primary approach described in this report by first building process maps in Microsoft Visio using templates that captured underlying information about the processes. We also designed Microsoft Excel spreadsheets that use exported data from Visio to calculate the total number of full-time equivalents (FTEs) required for each function. Although, in this report, we discuss the calculations that these tools perform, we avoid granular details about the makeup of the tools and the estimates that they produced in this particular application. Separate unpublished reports provided this information to the service in the form of a user guide and a white paper summarizing findings and limitations for each function.

An Outline of This Report

Chapter Two describes the general methods available and discusses the rationale behind the ones we chose to use in this staffing study. Chapter Three describes the primary and secondary approaches in more detail while highlighting some key considerations in implementing these approaches for the APT functions in the Secret Service. We dedicate Chapter Four to alternative approaches for IT functions, given the differences between common workflows in IT and those in other APT work. The report concludes with a discussion of potential refinements and lessons learned for future workforce planning efforts that are broadly applicable to federal agencies facing challenges similar to those at the Secret Service.

CHAPTER TWO

Selecting the Right Staffing Model

The term *model* might conjure up images of complex simulations brimming with quantitative rigor. In designing a model to inform staffing decisions, however, the approach that is appropriate for a given organization could involve no more than multiplication and addition. The information incorporated into a staffing model might not even be purely quantitative: Many approaches blend quantitative metrics with qualitative judgments about how to best accomplish the organization's mission. In this chapter, we survey the general approaches that we considered and describe the contextual factors in the Secret Service that informed our choice of the primary approach to developing the staffing models for the five Secret Service APT functions. After discussing general approaches, we describe our choice of approach in light of the organizational structure; workflows; available data sources; and organizational needs, such as ease of implementation and adaptability.

Planners Can Use Any of a Variety of Methods for Determining Staffing Needs

Determining the right level of staffing for a function requires an understanding of how workers generate outputs that are important to the organization. At its most basic level, then, a staffing model is a simplified representation of the work processes by which a function turns inputs (worker effort, technology, or other resources) into outputs (Figure 2.1). A model that faithfully represents the major features of the work can calculate the number of workers required to produce

Figure 2.1
Diagram of a Generic Staffing Model

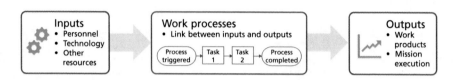

any desired level of output. Modeling decisions about how to represent the work processes and outputs give rise to different approaches for creating staffing models.

Staffing models can be grouped into four broad categories: (1) performance estimator models, (2) workload estimator models, (3) relative comparison models, and (4) business-case analysis (BCA) models (Broyles et al., unpublished research). In the first two categories, methods exist to model the work activities from the bottom up or in aggregate from the top down.

The selection of the most appropriate staffing model depends mainly on four factors: (1) data, (2) complexity, (3) uniqueness, and (4) business and management objective. For instance, a performance estimator model needs an organization (or a function) to define and collect performance data on its work processes. If performance data are not available, the organization can attempt to use workload estimator models. If the work is relatively simple in terms of the number of unique processes and the work activities performed, the organization can use the bottom-up approach to develop a performance estimator model or a workload estimator model. If the work is complex, mapping out the specific work activities could become untenable and the organization could turn to a top-down approach. If multiple locations are executing the same or similar work processes, the organization can apply relative comparison models that benchmark the level of staffing in the study function against comparison entities that are known to be appropriately staffed. If management has specific objectives or goals, the organization can use a BCA model to estimate its staffing needs. The requirement for multiple locations excludes relative comparison models from the suite of options for the current application. The rest of this section describes in more detail the methodological options that are in play for the five Secret Service study functions.

Performance Estimator Models

A performance estimator model links staff levels to output using data on how varying levels of staffing contribute to higher or lower performance, according to metrics, such as customer satisfaction or lead time. Therefore, as stated earlier, a performance estimator model requires that the organization define and collect performance data on its outputs. Figure 2.2 illustrates this concept by showing a notional relationship between the staffing level (on the horizontal axis) and the performance level (on the vertical axis). The data points could be the same office at different points in time, or they could represent distributed offices performing the same function. Alternatively, the data points could be simulated results from what-if scenarios run through a model of the workflow. The key feature of the performance estimator model is that the relationship shown in Figure 2.2 forms the basis of a staffing model that workforce planners would use to determine the staffing level that should achieve the organization's performance goals.

A significant advantage of performance estimator models is that they quantify the performance benefits of adequate staffing. However, performance estimator models are feasible under only certain narrow conditions. Applying a performance estimator model requires either detailed data on the relationship between staffing levels and performance, from which to estimate the statistical relationship shown in Figure 2.2, or a highly structured workflow that could be mathematically simulated while varying the staffing inputs (one example of such a simulation approach would be a queuing model, and Chapter Four provides a sample application of such a method). If these conditions do not exist, the alternative class of workload estimator models would calculate the number of staff that a function requires in order to accomplish the total workload for which the function is responsible.

Workload Estimator Models

Workload estimator models link staffing with work outputs or products rather than performance metrics. A workload estimator model

Figure 2.2
An Illustration of an Example Performance Estimator Staffing Model

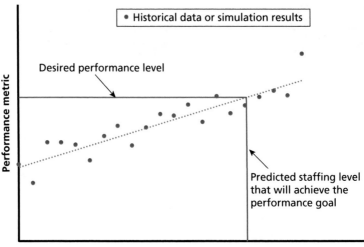

Number of APT staff per capita

then calculates the required staffing level using an estimate of the average level of worker productivity. To illustrate the distinction, consider an HR function responsible for enrolling new employees. A performance estimator model might use simulation results to calculate the number of staff required to ensure that the cycle time for processing new employees meets an organizational performance standard. A workload estimator model, on the other hand, might calculate the number of staff required to process all new employees using estimates of the time it takes for the average employee to accomplish all of the steps in the onboarding process.

Top-Down and Bottom-Up Approaches

There are two classes of approaches for representing the work processes that translate staffing inputs into either performance or workload outputs: top-down approaches and bottom-up approaches (Nataraj et al., 2014). Top-down approaches are the simpler of the two: They keep the link between staffing and outputs aggregated and use historical variation in staffing and workload drivers to derive the level of staffing needed in the future. Such models work well in cases in which work processes are consistent over time and historical staffing levels produced satisfactory performance. In cases in which processes or the organization changed significantly or historical staffing levels were not adequate, top-down approaches would be unreliable because the historical information would not be directly applicable to the future work environment (Broyles et al., unpublished research).

The alternative class of approaches, known as bottom-up approaches, begins with detailed estimates of the work required for each output, which can then be aggregated to form a staffing requirement for each function. Often, the backbone of a bottom-up staffing approach is a process-oriented description (or, more simply, a process map), which "is designed to document functions by inputs, process, and outputs, and then identify the subcomponents or details of these process elements" (National Research Council, 2013, p. 46). Process maps or other inputs capturing the essential steps in generating a function's outputs can form the basis of a mathematical model relating inputs to performance. Alternatively, process maps can be combined with estimates of the average time for each step and estimates for the number of process repetitions in a given time period to derive the total workload (in person-hours) that is required under different scenarios. Staffing models that use the bottom-up approach are intuitive, easily adaptable, and useful for general workforce planning purposes other than deriving staffing estimates (which we discuss in Chapter Five). The prime disadvantage of bottom-up approaches is that they can be time-consuming to build (for both the study team and the workers being studied), and this tediousness creates the risk that portions of the workload might be unintentionally omitted from the model and therefore can underestimate staffing requirements (Broyles et al., unpublished research).

Business-Case Analysis

In some areas of APT work, processes are so unstructured that significant features of the workflow cannot be adequately represented by a mathematical model or even an input–output process map. In these cases, the only available approach is to use qualitative staffing estimates derived from discussions with managers and SMEs. This type of approach is referred to as "direct managerial surveys" (Nataraj et al., 2014) or "business case analyses" (Broyles et al., unpublished research). These techniques assume that a manager of unstructured work is in the best position to assess their workforce needs and gaps. To form a picture of the gap between current and ideal staffing levels in a function, managers' opinions on required staffing levels can further be combined with indicators of understaffing (such as overtime use and work backlogs [National Research Council, 2013]) and subjective estimates regarding tasks that are required but not currently being executed because of staffing constraints.

The Bottom-Up Workload Estimator Approach Is the Most Suitable Basis for the Staffing Models in the Functions Under Study

The Secret Service APT functions that we studied vary in the types of work they perform and the scale of their operations. The Benefits and Payroll Division and the Administrative Operations Division are on one end of the complexity spectrum: Both functions perform administrative processes that tend to be relatively straightforward to map. In contrast, the Applications Development Branch performs technological operations that apply "agile" project management practices that are iterative in nature. The workflows in the Budget Division are somewhere in the middle, in that the process of formulating a budget is linear and amenable to process mapping but the steps in the process are complex and open-ended. In addition to having varying levels of workflow complexity, the study functions vary in size, ranging from 14 FTEs in the Budget Division to 57 FTEs in the Administrative Operations Division. Table 2.1 provides an overview of the studied functions.

The bottom-up workload estimator approach is the most suitable for this application, given that workflow structures and available data precluded performance estimator models, while the twin factors that these functions are unique in the organization and that the work has

Table 2.1
An Overview of the Studied Functions

Function	Organizational Component	Responsibility	Approximate Number of FTEs
Financial administration	Administrative Operations Division	Manage service properties and facilities.	57
	Budget Division, with distributed personnel	Formulate and execute budgets and provide program analysis and evaluation.	14
HR	Benefits and Payroll Division	Administer compensation and related programs for the Secret Service workforce.	30
IT, under the chief information officer	Applications Development Branch	Develop and maintain technical software applications: (1) the application services, (2) data services, and (3) special advisers.	48
	Communications Branch	Manage installations, maintenance, and accounts for voice, wireless, and radio communication.	50

changed significantly in recent years rule out relative comparison and top-down approaches.

Our strategy for choosing the right approaches evaluated the appropriateness of the candidate approaches for the five APT functions at the Secret Service in light of the organizational structure, workflows, available data, and operational needs. We also weighed the amount of quantitative precision that was feasible in light of other factors, such as ease of implementation and whether the approach could be easily adapted to future changes in workflow or organization. Our goal was for the Secret Service HR staff to maintain and apply the staffing models and tools we have developed for these functions. These factors point to the bottom-up approach as a clear choice for our primary modeling approach.

We explored opportunities to utilize performance estimator models, but none of our functions had existing performance data that could be used for modeling. Performance data measuring the response times to customers, customer satisfaction, or the accuracy or quality of work products were generally unavailable or had limitations that precluded use in a staffing model. For example, a portion of the workload for the Applications Development and Communications Branches is tracked in the ticketing system, which could yield information on how quickly customers see their issues resolved. However, we received consistent feedback that it is common for customers to bypass the ticketing system and that the time stamps in the system did not have enough detail to inform a model of the workflow.[1] Even if we had discovered performance metrics, however, historical data linking staffing to performance were unlikely to be informative, given the organizational changes that have taken place in recent years.[2]

Thus, the most appropriate modeling approach is a workload estimator model rather than a performance estimator model. After we determined this fact, the next decision involved whether to model the workflows from the bottom up or the top down. Because a top-down approach relies on deriving the historical relationship between the number of workers required and measures of workload, we dismissed this option for the same reasons of data limitations and organizational changes that prevented us from adopting the performance estimator approaches. Ultimately, then, the only approach that was flexible enough to meet the current need of creating a model "from scratch" was to estimate the workload from the bottom up.

Although modeling options were limited, the bottom-up approach has advantages for the current context. The components of a bottom-up model, which are essentially flowcharts of a function's work processes and spreadsheets performing multiplication and addition, do not require specialized training to understand and implement (unlike a statistical or simulation model). Furthermore, our discussions with

---

[1]   The ticketing system captures the open and close dates and times of maintenance issues but not the time that specialists are actively working on the issues. Chapter Four contains further discussion on this topic.

[2]   In addition to historical data on a single office, data linking staffing at multiple offices to performance might be useful in other contexts. Some organizations have distributed offices that perform the same function, and those offices can therefore be compared with one another. However, each of the Secret Service functions that we studied was a single office located at headquarters—one of a kind and performed only at the central location.

SMEs indicated that many of the sections within the studied functions are significantly understaffed for their assigned workloads. The downstream effects of understaffing can include significant overtime use and underexecution of the workload. This situation favors the bottom-up approach because it can account for tasked work that is not currently being accomplished or key steps that workers cannot currently perform because of understaffing.

Implementing a bottom-up approach required many tactical decisions, and a summary of these will be informative to service stakeholders and broader audiences. In Chapter Three, we describe these considerations, along with considerations in implementing BCAs, which we used as a complementary approach where appropriate.

CHAPTER THREE

Considerations for Implementing Our Primary and Secondary Approaches

This chapter provides more detail on how, once we had selected the bottom-up approach as the primary building block for our staffing models, we applied the approach and some key considerations in implementing it. We also provide more detail on our secondary approach, BCA, which is helpful either as a supplement to a model based on the bottom-up approach or in areas in which workflows did not permit the application of a bottom-up approach.

Our Primary Approach: Executing a Bottom-Up Workload Estimator Model

The distinctive feature of a bottom-up approach is that it begins by estimating the labor required for individual pieces of work and then aggregates all the separate pieces to form a staffing requirement for a function (Nataraj et al., 2014). Figure 3.1 is a conceptual diagram of the elements of our particular implementation of the bottom-up approach. Our default tool for representing individual pieces of work is the process-oriented description (or, more simply, process map), which breaks down the steps required to generate each of a function's outputs. We built process maps for each function through iterative discussions with the personnel in the various sections.[1] Once a function's

---

[1] In this report, *division* refers specifically to a division-type component of the organization (e.g., the Workforce Planning Division). Because some of the components we studied were branches rather than divisions, we use the generic term *function* to refer to the study com-

Figure 3.1
A Conceptual Diagram of Our Bottom-Up Workload Approach

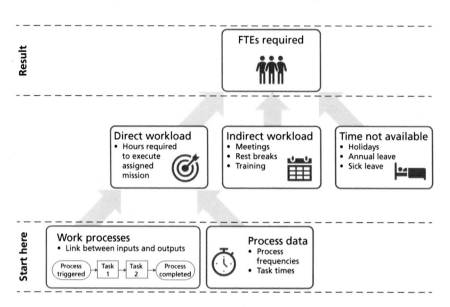

work processes were completely enumerated, we calculated the overall workload by combining these process maps with estimates of the frequency with which the function is required to execute each process and the time required to execute each task in the process. We express the workload as the average number of person-hours of work required per month. The work processes capture only the time required to execute the direct mission of the function; other necessary work activities that also require employee time (in the figure, denoted as "indirect workload"). We also accounted for employee absences due to, for example, vacation or sick leave. The final estimate for the number of FTE staff required to accomplish the function's responsibilities combines the direct workload with factors capturing indirect work and the average amount of time employees are unavailable to work.

In executing the bottom-up approach, the study team was dependent on personnel working in the sections to supply information about

---

ponents. Within a function, several subunits might be doing different things, and those are what we call *sections*.

the work processes that they perform. In general, we formulated initial process maps by interviewing the personnel who performed the work, then incorporated the views of section chiefs and managers who also provided valuable inputs. Hereafter, we refer to these personnel collectively as SMEs. These two vantage points of those who perform the work and those who oversee it can provide rich information in cases in which the current processes are not optimal. For example, managers often articulated a planned or desired process that differed from current operations, and our approach enabled us to incorporate both aspects into the staffing model and calculate the difference in the numbers of FTEs generated by the process reform effort (a use of the staffing models that is discussed in more detail in Chapter Five).

The Appropriate Level of Granularity for Process Maps

A key consideration when constructing a process map is ensuring that it captures the essential features of the work without excessive detail. For a few reasons, our approach was to strive for as much generality as possible. The most practical reason is that excessive detail requires additional SME time beyond what is already a labor-intensive process. More-general process maps are also easier to interpret, apply, refine, and change if processes or technology changes in the future. Furthermore, creating general process maps can also be more efficient: It allows for similar processes in different sections to be grouped together. To determine the right balance, we relied on collaboration with the SMEs for guiding the most effective way to represent the work.

Another factor in the granularity of the process maps involves the way the maps will ultimately interact with the process frequencies and task times to form the workload estimate. Any task that is too general will create difficulties in estimating the task time (which we describe further in the next section). For instance, the amount of work involved in a task could vary depending on circumstances, and this usually results in the addition of more structure in the process map to capture the different circumstances and the subtasks involved in each case. For example, Figure 3.2 shows the process map for the payroll activities involved in executing a military buyback, which occurs when an employee decides to apply their military service time toward

Figure 3.2
A Process Map of Payroll Military Buyback Activities

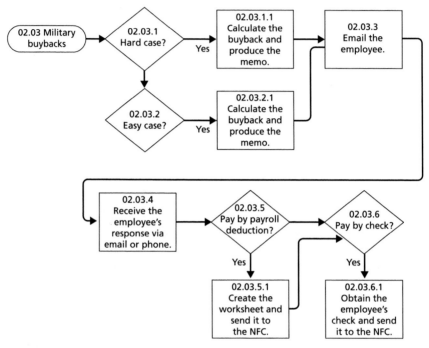

NOTE: NFC = National Finance Center.

their civil service retirement. For this process, SMEs indicated that estimating the time involved in calculating the buyback was difficult because the effort varied depending on how hard the case was. To help SMEs capture this variation, we represented hard versus easy cases as diamond-shaped decision nodes, which allowed the SMEs to provide separate time estimates in each case. Still, the fact that calculating the buyback is a single task reflects our goal of striving for generality: This task could be represented with multiple steps. In this case, such granularity was not necessary for the SMEs to represent the key features of the work.

An Estimation of Process Frequencies and Task Times

A bottom-up model that does not faithfully capture the work processes will not produce accurate staffing estimates. However, even a perfect set of process maps will be of little use without accurate estimates of the process frequencies and task times. Although the most convenient way to gather this information is from the SMEs who own the processes, overreliance on SME estimates could introduce significant error into the models because of known biases affecting task time recollection (Teter, 2014; Roy, Christenfeld, and Jones, 2013; Roy and Christenfeld, 2008; Roy and Christenfeld, 2007; Goswami and Urminsky, 2014). For this reason, our preferred option was to estimate frequencies and times from available data. When data are not available on critical tasks, another option is for SMEs to track the time required to execute the tasks if feasible within the project time frame. As a last resort, we relied on SME estimates, which lowered the fidelity of the resulting staffing estimates. However, as we discuss in Chapter Five, one of the uses of a bottom-up model could be to point to tasks with large contributions to the staffing estimates so that workforce planners can prioritize those tasks for future data collection.

Figure 3.3 shows the same process map as that in Figure 3.2 but with time and frequency estimates. These pieces represent the building blocks that will be aggregated to form the FTE estimate for the section. According to the annotated process map in Figure 3.3, the function performs 14 military buybacks per month. Multiplying the average frequency by the average duration of all tasks, weighted by the percentages in the decision nodes, yields a workload of about 93 hours per month, which amounts to 0.6 FTE.

When collecting estimates of process frequencies from SMEs, our general approach was to ask for the average frequency over the time frame that was most intuitive to the SME (e.g., daily, weekly) and rescale all frequencies to the monthly time frame in the background of the spreadsheet. For task durations, we asked SMEs to estimate the average amount of time required. In cases in which SMEs disagreed on a frequency or duration estimate, we relied on collaboration and discussion to resolve the issue, usually during the final calibration step discussed at the end of this chapter. More-formal and more-structured methods

Figure 3.3
A Process Map of Payroll Military Buyback Activities with Frequency and Time Estimates

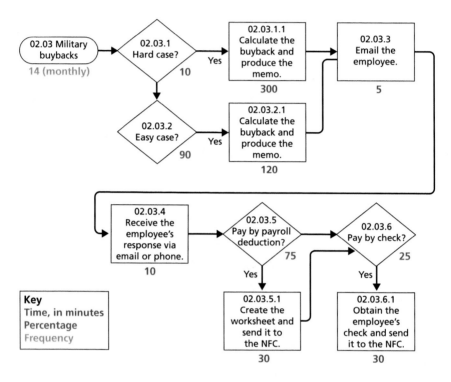

exist for collecting and consolidating quantitative estimates from multiple SMEs, such as RAND's Delphi method (Dalkey and Helmer-Hirschberg, 1962), but such methods were not practical here, given the large volume of estimates needed to complete a single bottom-up model.

If a function is understaffed, the current operations might differ from how the function would operate if it had more resources. Employees might delay some processes (such as a periodic policy review) in favor of higher priorities, which would affect the process frequency, or employees might rush or cut corners, which would affect the task times. To avoid enshrining the less-than-ideal operations into the staffing model, in cases in which the ideal differed from current operations, we collected both the current and planned (or desired) process frequencies and task times.

Highly Variable Task Times

A common challenge that emerged in discussions with SMEs involved how to capture open-ended tasks with variable times. For example, support functions often include open-ended consultation with customers, IT workers must troubleshoot issues of varying difficulty, and software developers might face a set of unique potential user requirements. There are three potential options for accounting for such situations in staffing models:

- **Use the average time.** In the end, resourcing the function based on the average task times will ensure enough staff to eventually accomplish the total workload. However, the average time could be difficult to estimate (in the case of SME estimates), and resourcing at the average level of effort might produce backlogs or high levels of overtime in the short run.
- **Build additional features into the process map.** If the time required to execute a task is so uncertain that SMEs cannot accurately estimate the average (and no data are available), key features that affect the task time can be incorporated into the process map. Figure 3.4 depicts a simplistic example involving software development in which certain software requests include advanced features requiring more developer labor but others require only baseline features. Breaking the efforts out into categories could help SMEs better estimate the level of effort required for each task. This practice could also improve the model's usefulness for planning because the distribution of features then becomes a model input that might vary in the future. Still, it is important to note that the resourcing decision in this example is based on the average time (i.e., ten person-days of effort), which could still lead to performance shortfalls (e.g., backlogs).
- **Further refine the model with performance standards.** The primary objection to the first two options might be that they could lead to unacceptable performance gaps in the short term. Man-

Figure 3.4
An Example of Incorporating Work Features into a Process Map

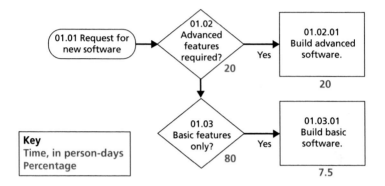

agers might prefer to resource above the average level of effort so that excess capacity is available for high-priority, mission-critical requests. In this case, a model based on total workload cannot give managers all the information needed to make a staffing decision because it does not account for these additional performance requirements. Managers could supplement the bottom-up model with additional business-case arguments concerning these performance standards or, if feasible and warranted, develop a performance estimator staffing model (e.g., a queuing or simulation model) to cover the variable portion of the workload.

Nonproductive Time and Availability to Work

The product of a set of process frequencies and the average times required to execute each step in the processes is the total workload of the function, usually expressed in the average number of person-hours required in a given time frame (e.g., monthly). To convert this value into FTEs, planners must also make assumptions about the amount of employee time that is allowed to go toward activities that do not directly contribute to the organizational outputs. Our approach for this was to create a factor for nonproduction time, calculated as the ratio of total time in a standard workweek to the productive time remaining after an assumed amount of time is subtracted to cover rest breaks, staff meetings, and organization-wide training. Using two daily 15-minute rest breaks, one weekly two-hour meeting, and 15 annual required training events of 1.5 hours each, we arrived at a factor of 1.14 for nonproduction time. We then scaled the original workload up by multiplying the person-hours required by the nonproduction factor, which adjusted the requirement for the additional time required for these activities.

Finally, determining the number of FTEs from a workload total in person-hours necessitates an assumption about the average number of hours that an FTE employee will be available to work. To capture this assumption, we created an availability factor by beginning with the total number of hours in a work-year (approximately 2,087 hours) and subtracting the number of hours that the average employee would be unavailable because of federal holidays (80 hours) and annual leave (160 hours). For other types of leave, we relied on information from the timekeeping system to calculate an average value for all APT employees, arriving at roughly 85 hours of sick leave per year and 29 hours of other forms of leave per year. Thus, the final availability factor assumes that one FTE will contribute 1,734 hours per year of work toward the person-hour requirement.

Fixed Position Requirements

Some positions within functions do not depend on the volume of work. For example, managers or section chiefs might be required for oversight, or a help desk position might need to maintain a 24/7 presence, regardless of the number of issues that come in. Our general approach was to take the organizational structure at face value, rather than estimating the requirements for managerial positions by analyzing their workload. For instance, wherever Secret Service managers indicated a need for a section chief, we plugged that position directly into the model as one FTE. However, the models include the flexibility for each fixed position to contribute a percentage of the time to accomplish the assigned workload if SMEs indicated that such work was within the scope of the position's responsibilities. We incorporated these percentages by subtracting the number of FTEs that the fixed positions contributed to the workload from the overall number of FTEs required to execute the workload.

National Special Security Events

One of the service's organizational responsibilities is to serve as the lead agency for security operations at special events of national significance, known as National Special Security Events (NSSEs). Some APT employees provide on-site support to NSSE activities, so we considered ways to account for this work requirement in the bottom-up staffing models. Although NSSE support is a unique responsibility of the Secret Service, the principles for how to account for irregular surges in workload readily generalize to other federal organizations.

We considered several options, as described in Table 3.1. Ultimately, determining which is the right approach or combination of approaches depends on how the organization plans to resource NSSE work. The common thread is that organizational managers face a trade-off with highly variable workloads in which maintaining excess capacity is helpful during an NSSE but inefficient during normal operations. The most efficient approach is to use a combination of overtime work and temporary and part-time workers to weather the NSSEs rather than hiring additional FTEs specifically for this work. Main-

Table 3.1
Potential Approaches for Resourcing National Special Security Events

Resourcing Decision	Model Approach	Potential Drawback
Absorb additional work through overtime or temporary workers or a combination of the two.	Ignore NSSE work in the FTE calculation.	This could result in unacceptably high overtime burdens, and temporary workers with correct skills might not be available.
Account for the long-run average NSSE workload.	Include NSSE time as a work process.	If regular work cannot be delayed, this approach results in too few FTEs during NSSEs unless they are supplemented with overtime and excess capacity otherwise.
Maintain excess staff to ensure minimum performance levels during NSSEs.	Set the number of FTEs at the NSSE requirement plus enough to meet the performance standard.	This requires a performance estimator model and results in excess capacity during normal operations.

taining additional FTE capacity during non-NSSE times to avoid performance degradation during NSSEs, if a manager so desires, would require a different staffing approach that quantifies the performance gains both during NSSEs and during normal operations. As noted previously, contextual factors in the functions that were the focus of this study hindered us from developing performance estimator models.

Among the five APT functions under study, three had at least some involvement in NSSEs. Figure 3.5 shows information from the timekeeping system comparing hours of NSSE support with hours of overtime charged for the function that had the greatest level of NSSE involvement (the figure depicts a single function for illustration purposes, but similar patterns existed in the other two functions).[2] First, Figure 3.5 illustrates that NSSE demands are highly irregular, meaning that simply resourcing the long-run average amount of time required

Figure 3.5
An Example of the Comparison Between the Number of Hours of Overtime Charged and the Number of Hours of National Special Security Event–Related Work Required

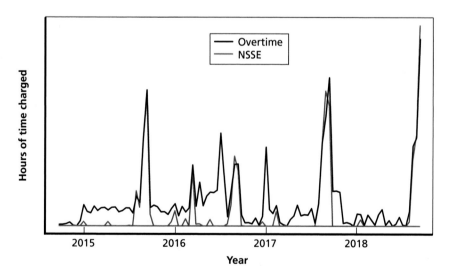

_____

[2]   Overtime and NSSE charges are not mutually exclusive in the timekeeping system.

would result in excess capacity most of the time while having a limited impact on the periodic surges in resource requirements for these events. Furthermore, for the NSSEs of the greatest magnitude, the amount of time required for NSSE work tracks very closely with overtime use, which suggests that current NSSE demands are met through authorization for overtime charges. Finally, after an NSSE event, the function returns to an equilibrium level of overtime in most cases, which suggests that the NSSE's effect on standard work is temporary. Using this information, we opted for a middle-ground version of the first option, in which we counted the time spent on NSSE work up to a maximum of the standard number of work-hours in a pay period, omitting the rest of the burden to be resourced by overtime use.

Our Secondary Approach: Business-Case Analysis

Although the bottom-up workload estimation approach has quantitative elements, it is not a purely quantitative method. Rather, bottom-up models are a way of quantifying leadership and SME judgments about the nature of a function's responsibilities and how best to achieve the organization's desired outcomes. Occasionally, an organization might need a staffing estimate in an area for which a bottom-up model is not feasible or practical, such as when the workflows are too open-ended or complex for a linear process map to reliably represent them. In such cases, the bottom-up models could be supplemented with BCAs. The term *BCA* has a variety of meanings in different contexts, but, in the area of staffing, it is a qualitative, gap-oriented exercise in which managers or SMEs provide an objective assessment of areas in which they are understaffed, overstaffed, or appropriately staffed.

As part of a BCA, SMEs should consider the current and future work environment (Emmerichs, Marcum, and Robbert, 2004a). The workload might be in flux or expected to increase in the future (likely the case for many APT functions because the law enforcement workforce they support is projected to grow). Then, SMEs should consider how the function's performance is measured and evaluate whether the current workforce is producing the right outcomes or levels of performance in their respective sections. The BCA method that we employed then asks SMEs to evaluate the workforce required to close current and future performance gaps, including an assessment of any work that is not currently being accomplished because of understaffing.

We also recommend use of a BCA as a supplement to a more quantitatively oriented model when the latter yields a significant difference between current workload and planned or desired workload and hence between current and planned or desired staffing levels. The BCA provides a rationale, linked to organizational objectives, for the planned or desired increase in workloads.

Our framework for a BCA includes the following elements:

- **background:** What is the mission of the function under study? How does this mission support the mission and objectives of the larger organizations of which it is a part?
- **activities:** What activities does the function undertake to support this mission?
- **current staffing:** How is the function currently organized and staffed?
- **performance and output gaps:** Are important objectives not being met at an acceptable level of performance? Are useful opportunities being missed? If so, which of these gaps, if any, are attributable to staffing limitations?
- **staffing objective:** If any performance or output gaps are attributable to staffing limitations, what additional staffing would be required to close the gaps? How was the additional staffing requirement determined?
- **assessment:** Are additional data, guidance, or other information needed to support the staffing objective? If additional staffing is needed, are other types of resources also needed to complement the additional staffing?

In developing or modifying a BCA for a function, two key linkages must be supported analytically:

- **the linkage between the function's outputs or outcomes and broader organizational objectives.** The current or potential value of the function's current, planned, or desired outputs or outcomes to leaders at higher organizational levels should be articulated. The analysis should allow senior leaders with resourcing authority to determine whether the resources currently devoted to or required for additional output from the function are warranted in view of competing demands for scarce resources.
- **the unit's staffing and its outputs or outcomes**, particularly the resources needed to close gaps in meeting organizational objectives. In less structured environments, this analysis tends to be very qualitative. However, the case for required resources is generally stronger if some quantitative analysis can be supplied.

Calibrating All Available Information to Arrive at a Staffing Estimate

Armed with a bottom-up representation of the workload in a function, a BCA that includes qualitative information about current performance gaps and necessary additional resources, or both, we proceeded to analyze the necessary staffing in each function as follows.

First, when using the current process frequencies and task times, the model should indicate no more or less than the current level of staffing. If the current data yield more than the current level of staffing plus the typical overtime burden,[3] the process frequencies or task times are likely overestimated. Alternatively, if the model projection based on current process frequencies and task times yields less than the current level of staffing, there should be evidence of slack time in the BCA. If managers indicate that the workforce is fully tasked, the process fre-

---

[3] We received information on overtime from the timekeeping system, but we also elicited perceptions on the typical amount of overtime from SMEs in case the timekeeping system did not fully account for overtime worked.

quencies or task times could be understated. In either case, this process of pegging the staffing estimate to the current workload could further highlight a need for data collection to better measure the level of effort required for processes or tasks that are responsible for relatively large contributions to the numbers of FTEs.

Even if the model appears well calibrated in aggregate, the underlying data could still have hidden inaccuracies. As an additional check, performing a qualitative review of the disaggregated work requirements is also beneficial. For example, SMEs could review the relative workload generated by each process and judge whether the results accord with personal experience. If SMEs report spending a relatively large amount of time working on a given process in light of that process's contribution to the staffing estimate, the frequencies or task times might need to be revisited.

Once the current workload appears to be well calibrated, the planned or desired process frequencies and task times provide an estimate of any necessary increases in staffing. The BCA could then contribute descriptive information about the additional performance that will result from the new resources called for in the staffing model, as well as serve as a qualitative check on the magnitude of the staffing increase. In this way, the BCA exercise is highly complementary to the process of modeling the workload from its individual elements.

In our work at the Secret Service, we accomplished these steps through one or more calibration meetings with each function's director or manager and relevant process owners. We started these sessions by confirming the current level of full-time staff in the section (including temporary and contract workers who contributed to the function's level of output) and showing our model application tool populated with initial process frequency and task time estimates. We first compared current estimated workload in FTEs with the stated workforce. Then, we showed the functional representatives the workload in FTEs generated by each process and compared these results with the SMEs' subjective impressions. This was the most intuitive way to present the information and thus the best way to generate refinements to the model parameters. For example, we often probed with a question along the following lines: "This process is measuring out to three FTEs of work. Do you currently have the equivalent of three employees working on this process full time?" If the answer to such probing questions was "no," we revised the process frequencies and task times to bring the estimates closer in line with the perceptions of those who performed the work.

Such discussions eventually brought the overall FTE estimate in line with the current workforce. We then proceeded to discuss each process and probe for whether the planned or desired workload differed from the current capacity so that we could adjust the process frequencies or task times accordingly. For example, some processes performed by the Benefits and Payroll Division, such as payroll actions, are driven by the overall size of the workforce. Thus, we scaled the process frequencies up proportionately according to the projected increases in the workforce from the current human capital strategic plan (U.S. Secret Service, 2017). The last step was to show the functional representatives the estimated increases in the number of FTEs for which the planned or desired workload called and compare this number with their subjective assessment of the resources needed to close their performance gaps.

CHAPTER FOUR

Alternative Approaches for Information Technology Functions

Many of the workflows in financial administration and HR conform well to a staffing approach based on process maps because the workflows progress from one stage to another and have clear starting and ending points. However, these approaches are not a good fit for the IT realm because the workflows involve handling unforeseen issues as they continuously arise at unpredictable intervals, or because they involve teams of developers building software of uncertain scope through an iterative process of discovering and refining the customer's needs. Such workflows are increasingly common in IT because of the spread of agile methodologies for project management. Agile methodologies emerged as a response to chronic problems associated with applying linear process management to software development. As IT increased in prominence in the 1990s, software development projects suffered high failure rates that were attributable to the practice of delivering software all at once via a predetermined plan with insufficient collaboration with end users (Cooke, 2012). In contrast to the linear project management methods (sometimes referred to as waterfall methods because they break development into sequential, serially dependent stages), agile methodologies stress incremental planning that adapts throughout the life of the project, as well as frequent customer interaction to ensure that the development focuses on the highest-priority features. Although it is possible to abstract an agile workflow into a linear process map for developing a staffing model, the misalignment of the model and the workflows could introduce additional error into the model. This chapter discusses additional methodologies for agile workflows, based on our experience in selecting an approach for the portion of the Secret Service's Applications Development Branch that develops and maintains software applications.[1]

Software Operations and Maintenance Activities

At the Secret Service, software operations and maintenance (O&M) activities are managed via an agile methodology known as kanban. Kanban is a way to manage and prioritize competing tasks for a group of specialists while limiting the amount of work to which each specialist commits, thereby ensuring that they can deliver business value. The hallmark of the method is the kanban board, which visualizes the status of all work, availability of specialists to take on additional work, and any obstacles to progress (Cooke, 2012). O&M activities at the Secret Service are managed via a digital kanban board in the workflow management system. This sort of workflow data is a crucial ingredient in creating a performance estimator staffing model.

The simplest way to calculate staffing needs for O&M, analogous to the bottom-up model calculations used elsewhere, would be to calculate a requirement based on the average number of maintenance issues in a given time frame and the average amount of labor required to resolve each maintenance issue. The fundamental limitation of this approach is that a staffing level that is sufficient for the average workload could still result in unacceptable performance or risk to the organizational mission. To illustrate this dynamic in staffing decisions, consider a simple example in which O&M requests pop up randomly and addressing the requests requires a varying amount of effort. In this example, the O&M staff receive three new requests per month, and fulfilling each request requires an average of ten standard workdays (or 80 person-hours) of effort, which means that one employee can com-

---

[1] This branch also performs other functions, for which we applied the bottom-up approaches described in earlier chapters.

plete 1.83 requests per month without working overtime.[2] Under some hypothetical assumptions about worker availability and indirect work, this function would require 1.8 FTEs, so a manager might staff the function with two full-time employees.

In reality, the number of requests will not be exactly three in each month, and each request might be different—some will take less than ten days, while others might take considerably longer. Another way to conceptualize this problem is to formulate it as a basic queuing system, which allows the number of requests and the time to resolution to vary while producing performance statistics. Table 4.1 illustrates the results of three scenarios if this function is modeled as a basic queuing system. Although two FTEs is enough manpower to accomplish all of the

Table 4.1
Sample Performance Statistics for Staffing a Request-Driven Workload of 1.8 Full-Time Equivalents

Statistic	Resource at Two FTEs	Resource at Two FTEs with 8 Hours per Person of Overtime per Month	Resource at Three FTEs
Average number of requests in backlog	3.4	2.4	0.3
Average time from request to resolution, in months	1.7	1.3	0.7
Percentage of time employees are working on requests	82	78	55

NOTE: Queuing results assume an arrival rate of three requests per month and a service rate of either 1.83 requests per month (based on ten days per request and the standard number of workdays in a month) or 1.93 requests per month (if an additional day of overtime is available). For simplicity, both interarrival and service times are assumed to follow exponential distributions. The calculations assume a baseline availability of 35 hours per week for productive work.

---

[2] This service rate is based on the 80-hour requirement and the assumption that the average employee is available to work 35 hours per week, on average (which translates into 146.37 hours per month). Dividing 146.37 hours of work per month by 80 hours per request produces a service rate of 1.83 requests per month.

function's workload, the queuing calculations indicate that the system would tend to have an average of 3.4 requests in backlog and that the customer would see an average time to resolution of 1.7 months, including the wait time. This level of performance might be unacceptably slow, or it might introduce risk to other IT systems that builds as maintenance issues sit unaddressed (Taber and Port, 2016). Thus, the organization might consider reducing the backlog and time to resolution through overtime or adding an additional FTE at the expense of a lower tendency to utilize the employees.

For determining the right staffing level for software O&M activities, the queuing approach is preferable to the average workload calculation because it explicitly models performance outcomes associated with the workflows. However, organizations (including the Secret Service) are often limited in their ability to implement this approach because (1) it requires detailed data on the number and timing of maintenance issues and the level of effort required to resolve them[3] and (2) it often requires a computer simulation for implementation (Broyles et al., unpublished research). Because we ultimately could not implement this approach at the Secret Service because of limitations in the availability of data (as discussed in Chapter Two), providing further detail on the methodology is outside the scope of this report. Interested readers should see Taber and Port, 2016, for a detailed example of a queue-based staffing model for software O&M activities.

Software Development Activities

In addition to O&M for existing IT systems, a function at the service oversees an organic capability to develop new software applications to meet mission needs. The workflow of software development activities across the IT industry has been heavily influenced by an agile framework known as scrum (Schwarber and Sutherland, 2017), which gov-

---

[3] An organization might need to intentionally collect this information because the ticketing system might record only the open and close dates and times associated with a request rather than the amount of time that specialists are continuously working to resolve an issue.

erns the workflow of this function at the Secret Service. In contrast to waterfall management techniques, in which development activities would follow a scheduled set of sequential steps, the scrum framework prescribes a workflow in which a nimble team of three to nine members produces the software through "sprints" that take no longer than one month each. Each sprint aims to produce an incremental piece of working software for the team and other stakeholders to review, with an opportunity to collect feedback and reprioritize remaining development activities or to change course. Scrum proponents posit that the end product of the many sprints tends to produce more value and has a lower risk of failure because the process ensures that the development work steadily progresses toward the user's requirements.

Designing a staffing approach for this workflow has two general elements: The organization must determine the scope of software development capability that is required as a basis for staffing decisions, and the approach must include a way to accommodate the constraints of the scrum framework, which affect how developers are utilized.

In the same way that workforce planners use judgment to determine the force presentation packages for SAs and UD officers, the organization first needs to determine the software development output level that will satisfy mission requirements. Because software development under the scrum framework is project based, planners would ideally define the outputs as a schedule of projects that need to be completed in a given time frame, with personnel requirements and necessary timelines that match the complexity of the projects. Determining the types of projects on which to base staffing requirements should be informed by data on recent demand or by the current backlog of projects awaiting execution. This project schedule then forms the basis for staffing calculations using one of several potential methods.

Like with O&M activities, the simplest approach to calculate staffing would be to total the person-hours of work required to execute the project schedule and convert this number to FTEs. For example, suppose that the function needs to produce three large applications; that the applications have project durations of four, six, and eight months; and that each application requires a four-person development team. This schedule would entail a total of 72 person-months of work per year. Depending on assumptions for vacation and sick leave, this workload would call for roughly seven FTEs in developer labor.[4] However, this simple example shows the potential pitfall inherent in this calculation: The scrum framework limits the size of a team and generally requires a team to focus on a single project. Thus, because seven FTEs is not enough to staff two complete teams, a staffing level of seven could introduce delays and some additional risk to the mission. Completing all three hypothetical applications in a year without deviating from the scrum framework requires two full four-person teams, or eight FTEs.

Therefore, one alternative to the simple workload calculation is to explicitly enumerate the desired outputs and posture staff requirements to produce those outputs, an approach that could be considered a form of position-based manning analogous to the standard force presentation packages of the law enforcement side of the service. However, continuing the example, if one were to staff the function at eight FTEs for the three projects, the organization would essentially need to justify four months of slack for one of the teams.[5]

To address this limitation, a third option that we propose is to formulate the staffing model for both O&M and software development as a constrained optimization program. Essentially, this approach would express the staffing question as a mathematical program that accepts the predefined project schedule and O&M requirements as demand inputs and solves for the minimum number of personnel required to meet the desired demand.[6] The scrum framework enters the problem as a series of mathematical constraints (e.g., ensuring that a developer works continuously on a single project until completion) to be combined with other constraints for O&M capacity (such as the minimum

---

[4]   For example, if each employee receives ten holidays, 20 days of paid vacation, and ten days of sick leave, then the simplest calculation would call for 6.8 FTEs.

[5]   This slack would not be an issue if the work were performed by contract teams that could be retained for only part of the year or if there were a continuous backlog of new projects that the additional team could take on.

[6]   We developed a test version of this model and implemented it as a mixed-integer program in the General Algebraic Modeling System for mathematical optimization.

number of personnel assigned to O&M that will ensure adequate performance according to the queuing model). The primary advantage of this approach is that it determines a staffing level under the structure of the scrum framework while allowing any slack that emerges to be applied to O&M work, thereby preventing the scrum structure from unnecessarily inflating the staffing estimate. Its primary disadvantages include the complexity of implementing it and the fact that it assumes a sort of optimal use of personnel that might be difficult to achieve in practice.

Applying These Methods to the Applications Development Branch

Among these options, the highest-fidelity staffing approach for the software activities in the Applications Development Branch would be to combine a queuing model of O&M activities with an optimization model that is informed by a detailed analysis of current and past workflows. Such a model would enable stakeholders to have a transparent discussion about the staffing required for the level of O&M performance and production that will meet mission needs. However, the current study was constrained by the available data in that (1) current practices do not track all O&M work in the ticketing system, (2) the ticketing system does not consistently record the time when developers are actively working the issues, and (3) data on new development workflows were not available to the research team. Because of these limitations, our approach for these activities relied on workload calculations that captured the average amount of O&M effort required to maintain each fielded application (according to SMEs) and the estimated project-based workload for new development activities, taking into account the desired team size and level of oversight. SMEs also provided inputs on the size and complexity of the project backlog so that we could estimate planned or desired levels of staffing that would accomplish this additional work within a time horizon specified by the organization.

Improving Staffing Approaches for Information Technology Functions

There is great potential for organizations, including the Secret Service, to implement staffing models for IT functions with a high degree of confidence because of the possibility of easy-to-collect workflow data. The first step toward improving staffing approaches for IT, then, is to confirm that workflow data are available and analyze the patterns of demand for O&M and new software development and the labor required to meet demand, as well as key performance statistics (such as time to resolution or average queue length). If the service were to collect and monitor those data, workforce planners might find that the workload estimator results are insufficient to meet organizational performance goals. Alternatively, workforce planners might find that SME judgments about the workload required for software development activities are imprecise and that some fine-tuning is necessary. In either of these cases, there are options for richer staffing approaches. The methods described in this chapter provide a way to quantify the likely performance level and level of mission risk inherent in different staffing decisions and recommend a staffing level that will achieve performance targets.

CHAPTER FIVE

Lessons Learned for Future Analyses of Staffing Needs

We close this report by emphasizing some lessons learned for future work based on challenges that we encountered in executing the current staffing study. We expect that these recommendations will help inform the design of future work at the Secret Service and in other federal agencies.

Certain Conditions Must Exist to Maximize the Benefit of a Staffing Study

In the planning process for the current study, we worked with Secret Service managers to prioritize the functions in the APT workforce according to their staffing needs. After embarking on the study using the list of predefined functions, the research team encountered many subareas in which preemptive policy adjustments could have significantly improved the degree of confidence in the resulting staffing estimates. A more effective strategy would be to attempt to discover such obstacles in a preliminary assessment and mitigate them before proceeding with the development of a staffing model (National Research Council, 2013). Thus, we recommend that future work include a preliminary assessment phase in which study teams have the opportunity to examine whether all of the following conditions are met. Where these conditions do not exist, the function should have the opportunity to implement changes before proceeding with a staffing study:

- **SMEs in the function have sufficient time to participate in the study.** A consistent limitation in conducting the current study was SME availability to provide inputs into the model development process. Our study functions rightly received priority because they were understaffed, but the unintended consequence of this decision was that time with functional SMEs was greatly constrained. To mitigate this challenge, we recommend that the organization make incremental staffing adjustments prior to model development or temporarily augment staffing in target functions to permit participation in the study.
- **Organizational structure and mission are clearly defined and stable.** An additional limitation in some sections in the functions under study was that the structure or mission of the sections was either in infancy or not established enough for model development. For example, some sections had recently received new responsibilities for processes and tasks, but it was not clear that the organization intended to resource those responsibilities permanently in those sections, calling into question whether they should be included in the staffing model. In cases in which recent changes have occurred to the organizational structure or mission of a function, we recommend either delaying the study until conditions stabilize or placing those sections outside of the study scope.
- **Work processes are stable and efficient.** One of the risks of the bottom-up approach is that it has the potential to harm organizational effectiveness by enshrining inefficient processes into the staffing estimates. Furthermore, we encountered some processes that were in flux and others that were entirely theoretical and had never been executed (because of understaffing). In such cases, it would be better to streamline and standardize the processes to ensure that they are stable before using them as a basis for a staffing model.

- **Workflow data on key processes are captured.** As discussed in Chapter Three, workflow data often exist, but this does not mean that the particular inputs needed for a staffing model are readily available. In such cases, it would be better for a function to adjust data collection procedures (or related policies, such as use of the ticketing system) and revisit a staffing model after data have had a chance to populate. Creating the opportunity to base a model on workflow data, as opposed to SME estimates, greatly increases the possibility for staffing estimates that come with a high degree of confidence and validity.
- **Function performance dimensions are defined and (if possible) captured in data.** A staffing model that is based on performance rather than total workload allows an organization to make a more compelling case for additional staffing by clearly articulating the performance shortfalls that could result from under-resourcing. However, many administrative functions collect no performance data that researchers can incorporate into staffing models. If possible, functions should define their performance metrics and begin collecting performance data prior to embarking on a staffing study.

Even Models with Limited Quantitative Precision Help Make Planning More Transparent

The most common reason organizations pursue staffing models is to objectively determine the number of FTEs that will be needed in a function, in a way that can be used to advocate for resources. The reality, however, is that it is sometimes impossible to produce a quantitatively precise staffing estimate for certain types of administrative work because of the structure of the workflows and the limitations in available data. For this reason, we designed our staffing tools so that workforce managers could use them for more-holistic planning decisions in three main areas (Figure 5.1). The tool that we designed (implemented as a Microsoft Excel spreadsheet) takes advantage of the tremendous amount of information inherent in a bottom-up model,

Figure 5.1
Bottom-Up Models Serve Multiple Workforce Planning Functions

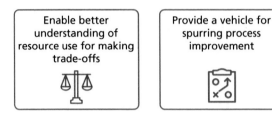
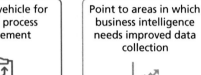

even one derived solely from SME inputs, which includes a complete enumeration of major work tasks and the effort required to execute them. First, by changing the process frequencies or task durations and observing the resulting changes in staffing levels, workforce managers can use the information in the model to perform what-if analysis and understand resource trade-offs. For instance, managers can readily calculate the amount of additional staff required to execute a process more frequently or, alternatively, the resource savings of eliminating or automating a process. Similarly, because the bottom-up models capture all work tasks for a function, managers can use them to explore the steps in the most labor-intensive work activities to identify areas in which there might be significant savings from process improvement. Last, managers could use the components of a bottom-up model to target business intelligence efforts, either to refine estimates of process frequencies or task durations that have a large impact on staffing levels or to monitor performance outputs alongside the workflow outputs captured in the model. Ultimately, even when bottom-up models of primarily administrative work cannot produce precise, quantitative forecasts, they can still be useful as tools that inject transparency into workforce planning, enabling managers to see the whole landscape of activities in a function and determine how much to resource and where to focus improvement efforts.

There Is Benefit to Focused Periods of Model Development

A key lesson from the current study involves how to best involve organization SMEs in the development of a staffing model. Our approach was essentially to attempt to study all functions in parallel while working around SME availability because this seemed like the most efficient approach to collect necessary inputs without affecting the organizational mission. This strategy turned out to be inefficient because the intermittency in SME contact forced the study team to duplicate effort—either to remind SMEs of work that had already been accomplished or to work through instances of employee turnover. We recommend that, going forward, the organization increase use of earmarked, focused blocks of time for model development coupled with plans to mitigate mission impacts so that SMEs can fully participate in the staffing study. If this is not possible, planners should consider whether an incremental staffing adjustment or a delay in the staffing study would be preferable to forcing SMEs to juggle study participation with an overly demanding work tempo.

Conclusion

Staffing models can take many forms depending on the organizational context, nature of the function's workflow, and available data. The goal of this report is to provide stakeholders of the Secret Service with a strategic overview of the methodological considerations and decisions we made in our effort to develop reliable staffing models for its five APT functions. We expect that, even though the report is targeted for the Secret Service, other federal agencies can also benefit from our methodological description to develop staffing models for their APT employees working in similar functions. Staffing models (especially the bottom-up variety) require significant investment in time and effort up front, but, once developed, they can often be continuously updated and (as discussed above) help in other resourcing and workforce planning decisions. No model can predict the future with certainty, but there is value added in making workforce planning decisions more transparent so that managers can be explicit about the trade-offs involved.

References

Broyles, James R., Shawn McKay, Albert A. Robbert, Kristin Van Abel, Maria DeYoreo, Cedric Kenney, and Kristin J. Leuschner, *Staffing Models for Customs and Border Protection's Support Services: A Methodology and Specific Applications*, Homeland Security Operational Analysis Center operated by the RAND Corporation, unpublished research.

Cooke, Jamie Lynn, *Everything You Want to Know About Agile: How to Get Agile Results in a Less-Than-Agile Organization*, Cambridgeshire, UK: IT Governance Publishing, 2012.

Dalkey, Norman Crolee, and Olaf Helmer-Hirschberg, *An Experimental Application of the Delphi Method to the Use of Experts*, Santa Monica, Calif.: RAND Corporation, RM-727/1, 1962. As of July 18, 2019:
https://www.rand.org/pubs/research_memoranda/RM727z1.html

Emmerichs, Robert M., Cheryl Y. Marcum, and Albert A. Robbert, *An Operational Process for Workforce Planning*, Santa Monica, Calif.: RAND Corporation, MR-1684/1-OSD, 2004a. As of September 3, 2019:
https://www.rand.org/pubs/monograph_reports/MR1684z1.html

———, *An Executive Perspective on Workforce Planning*, Santa Monica, Calif.: RAND Corporation, MR-1684/2-OSD, 2004b. As of September 3, 2019:
https://www.rand.org/pubs/monograph_reports/MR1684z2.html

GAO—*See* U.S. Government Accountability Office.

Goswami, Indranil, and Oleg Urminsky, "More Time, More Work: How (Incidental) Time Limits Bias Estimates of Project Time and Scope," in June Cotte and Stacy Wood, eds., *Advances in Consumer Research*, Vol. 42, Duluth, Minn.: Association for Consumer Research, 2014, pp. 86–90. As of September 3, 2019:
http://www.acrwebsite.org/volumes/v42/acr_v42_17606.pdf

Hagin, Joseph, Thomas Perrelli, Danielle Gray, and Mark Filip, *Executive Summary to Report from the United States Secret Service Protective Mission Panel to the Secretary of Homeland Security*, Washington D.C.: U.S. Department of Homeland Security, December 15, 2014. As of September 3, 2019:
https://www.dhs.gov/publication/
executive-summary-report-usss-protective-mission-panel

Nataraj, Shanthi, Christopher Guo, Philip Hall-Partyka, Susan M. Gates, and Douglas Yeung, *Options for Department of Defense Total Workforce Supply and Demand Analysis: Potential Approaches and Available Data Sources*, Santa Monica, Calif.: RAND Corporation, RR-543-OSD, 2014. As of September 21, 2018:
https://www.rand.org/pubs/research_reports/RR543.html

National Academy of Public Administration, *United States Secret Service: Review of Organizational Change Efforts*, Washington, D.C.: Academy Project 2204, October 31, 2016. As of September 3, 2019:
https://www.napawash.org/studies/academy-studies/
united-states-secret-service-review-of-organizational-change-efforts

National Research Council, *Assessment of Staffing Needs of Systems Specialists in Aviation*, Washington, D.C.: National Academies Press, 2013. As of September 3, 2019:
https://www.nap.edu/catalog/18357/
assessment-of-staffing-needs-of-systems-specialists-in-aviation

Public Law 107-296, Homeland Security Act of 2002, November 25, 2002. As of May 12, 2019:
https://www.govinfo.gov/app/details/PLAW-107publ296

Roy, Michael M., and Nicholas J. S. Christenfeld, "Bias in Memory Predicts Bias in Estimation of Future Task Duration," *Memory and Cognition*, Vol. 35, No. 3, April 2007, pp. 557–564.

———, "Effect of Task Length on Remembered and Predicted Duration," *Psychonomic Bulletin and Review*, Vol. 15, No. 1, February 2008, pp. 202–207.

Roy, Michael M., Nicholas J. S. Christenfeld, and Meghan Jones, "Actors, Observers, and the Estimation of Task Duration," *Quarterly Journal of Experimental Psychology*, Vol. 66, No. 1, 2013, pp. 121–137.

Schwarber, Ken, and Jeff Sutherland, "The Scrum Guide: The Definitive Guide to Scrum—The Rules of the Game," Scrum Guides, November 2017. As of May 28, 2019:
https://www.scrumguides.org/scrum-guide.html

Taber, William, and Dan Port, "Staffing Strategies for Maintenance of Critical Software Systems at the Jet Propulsion Laboratory," *ESEM '16: Proceedings of the 10th ACM/IEEE International Symposium on Empirical Software Engineering and Measurement*, 2016, art. 49.

Teter, Michael, *Applying Subject Matter Expert (SME) Elicitation Techniques to TRAC Studies*, Monterey, Calif.: U.S. Army Training and Doctrine Command Analysis Center, TRAC-M-TR-14-036, September 30, 2014. As of September 3, 2019:
https://apps.dtic.mil/docs/citations/ADA616463

U.S. Code, Title 6, Domestic Security; Chapter 1, Homeland Security Organization; Subchapter III, Science and Technology in Support of Homeland Security; Section 185, Federally Funded Research and Development Centers. As of May 12, 2019:
https://www.govinfo.gov/app/details/USCODE-2017-title6/
USCODE-2017-title6-chap1-subchapIII-sec185

U.S. Government Accountability Office, *High-Risk Series: Substantial Efforts Needed to Achieve Greater Progress on High-Risk Areas*, Washington, D.C., GAO-19-157SP, March 6, 2019. As of September 3, 2019:
https://www.gao.gov/products/GAO-19-157SP

U.S. Secret Service, *FY 2018–FY 2025 Human Capital Strategic Plan*, Washington, D.C.: Offices of Strategic Planning and Policy, Human Resources, and the chief financial officer, May 2017.